GLιMMER

Of

HOPE

Sandra Mills

WALDENHOUSE PUBLISHERS, INC.
WALDEN, TENNESSEE

A GLIMMER of HOPE

ISBN: 978-1-947589-46-9
Library of Congress Control Number: 2021947867
True story of a woman's experience with domestic abuse, her escape and recovery. Many helpful suggestions are given for those who are considering a relationship with a person with abusive tendencies or who are already in an abusive relation-ship. ~ provided by Publisher
Published by Waldenhouse Publishers, Inc.
100 Clegg Street, Signal Mountain, Tennessee, USA 37377
423-886-2721   www.waldenhousepublishers.com
Printed in the United States of America
SEL001000 SELF-HELP / Abuse
SEL023000 SELF-HELP / Personal Growth / Self-Esteem
SEL032000 SELF-HELP / Spiritual

Dedication

To
All who have experienced the trauma
of domestic violence, either directly or indirectly

You are not alone.
The suffering of physical and psychological abuse
afflicts nearly every corner of our society.

This book is intended to help victims avoid,
survive, escape, and recover from every wound
inflicted by the abusers of this world.

To Nancy

From
Sandra Mills

A Glimmer of Hope

Table of Contents

A Glimmer of Hope

Acknowledgments

Sincere thanks to the following women who helped me prepare this book for publication by thoroughly reading the text, editing it, and making valuable suggestions for changes, for which I am deeply grateful: Jessica Ginese, Christina Henderson, Donna Sellers, and Julie Stansel.

I also thank Rose Brandt for the many hours of typing my oral story into printed text. Her work and dedication in helping me complete this task means so much to me.

Above all, I thank my Lord for guiding me through the most difficult times of my life and for bringing me back from hopelessness to a life of joy and peace. I thank Him for inspiring me to write this story and for allowing me to see it though completion.

A Glimmer of Hope

Preface

There are many reasons why women are in abusive situations. It is impossible to describe all the thoughts that race through the minds of those who are being victimized.

An abuser tricks and traps them by creating a web of multiple kinds of abuse. The victims discover they have been woven into a tight knot that is extremely dangerous to escape. Most victims do not "decide" to stay, and it can be very risky to "just pick up and leave."

No one wants to be abused. It becomes a matter of survival. By sharing the story of my life, I hope I can help the many women who are currently being abused or who have been abused in the past. I especially hope that some women will be able to avoid the trap of domestic violence.

Regardless of the traumatic treatment you are enduring or have endured, I offer you the hope that you can survive this and live to see a better day. If I had not lived through every minute of abuse, escape, and recovery, I would never have believed that my life could have turned out as well as it has.

I thank God for His mercy and grace in helping me survive and for bringing me to the happy and peaceful life that I now live. There is hope for you, too. Thanks to God's great love for you, He will shine a light on the path of your deliverance from abuse. Maybe, just maybe, this book will provide a few steps in the right direction for your escape and recovery. That is my prayer for you.

A Glimmer of Hope

CHAPTER ONE:

MY FAMILY BACKGROUND

DISCLAIMER: I do not remember my father, but I do recall the many stories I was told about him and my family's early years. These are some of my favorite memories.

Daddy was a kind and smart young man who grew up in Ft. Payne, Alabama, in a wealthy family. His family owned a large farm, gas station, bank, and grocery store. After high school, he attended West Point Military Academy and then joined the U.S. Army during World War I. After the war, he and his brother shared the responsibility of running the family-owned businesses, which they later inherited.

Daddy took over the grocery store and the gas station in Ft. Payne. He always had a tender heart for people, though sometimes too tender. During the depression days, he allowed people to put groceries and gas on their "tab." Eventually he lost both the store and the gas station mainly because too many people failed to pay him back as they had originally agreed. Fortunately, he did not lose everything. He still owned part of the large family farm.

Things were going well on the farm when Daddy got serious about entering the world of politics. He ran for a seat in the Alabama senate and had a good chance of winning. He put the farm up as collateral to pay the expenses of the campaign. Unfortunately, he lost the election by four votes and the farm in the process. Daddy was still kind, smart and generous, but he was no longer wealthy.

Mama's childhood years were much different from Daddy's. Her mother died when Mama was only ten years old. Mama's father remarried soon after his wife died. His new wife was a widow who already had thirteen children. She was extremely busy taking care of her own children and did not want to add another child. She encouraged Mama to get married at the young age of fifteen and go live elsewhere.

Mama married a nice school friend (Wyler) who was also a teenager. The next few years were terribly hard for them both. They had two little boys right away (Roy and Russell). Their family life centered around activities at Gravel Hill Baptist Church in Cobrun, Alabama, just outside Ft. Payne. Mama and Wyler had both attended this church since childhood. They were given great physical and spiritual support at that church.

Unfortunately, when the boys were just toddlers, Mama's young husband died from double pneumonia at the age of nineteen. This left Mama heartbroken, empty-handed, and alone with her two young sons.

During this time, Daddy was also a long-time member of Gravel Hill Baptist Church. He saw all the sad difficulties that Mama was going through. Even though Daddy was seventeen years older than Mama, his tender heart felt a great compassion toward her. She was a beauty and had even been crowned Miss

Attalla, Alabama. That is when he began calling her "the most beautiful woman in Alabama."

He was ready to rescue her from her young widowhood and help her raise her two boys. They began dating and were married a few weeks later in December 1920. Although he was 37, and she was only 20 years old, the family was excited and happy for them.

Their big house in Ft. Payne became filled with little children over the next twenty years. Daddy was raising Roy (1916) and Russell (1918) as his very own, and then they had eleven more children while living there. Their first child was Betty (1921), then Robert Alexander (1922), Margaret (1925), Sam (1926), Essie Lucille (1928), Mary Jo (1928), Rose (1930), Imojean (1933), Addie Kay (1935), Ralph Melvin (1937), and finally Marion Ralph (1938). Sadly, Margaret, Essie Lucille, and Ralph Melvin all died less than a month after their births.

The Ft. Payne home was a busy place. They had a long table with enough benches and chairs for everyone to eat together. There were three big bedrooms where the girls shared the old-fashioned iron beds. Since the house was in town, they were able to walk to both school and Gravel Hill Baptist Church.

When Daddy retired from the U.S. Army, he accepted a government job at the Army depot in Gadsden, Alabama. The family moved everything they had from Ft. Payne down to Gadsden to another large house with four long porches going nearly around the entire house. I was born on September 19, 1941, and was the last of fourteen children born to my parents.

To say that I was spoiled by all my older siblings would be an understatement. In fact, my nickname quickly became "Spoiled Brat." Life was good for our big family. Eventually some of the older siblings moved to other cities, while those who remained at home continued to help Mama with the littlest ones. Marion and I were well loved and cared for by our big brothers and sisters. Although we were poor, there was always enough to make it through.

One morning in 1946, everything changed. Mama discovered that Daddy had died during the night from a massive heart attack. I do not remember much about it, but I do recall the casket being brought to our house for several days before the funeral. He was 65. Mama was a widow yet again, this time at age 47, with six children still at home to raise. I was only five years old.

My oldest brother, Roy, and my oldest sister, Betty, both lived in Chattanooga, Tennessee. After things settled down, Betty suggested to Mama that we should move from Gadsden to Chattanooga, so that they could help with the children. A year later, we moved to Chattanooga to a little house across the street from my cousins.

Our family quickly became active at Temple Baptist Church. I really enjoyed being there and have many happy memories of those days. Brother Talley was our pastor, and Mr. Keith was my Sunday School teacher. I had always loved to sing, so when I was thirteen, I joined the choir. I accepted Jesus as my personal Savior one Sunday night at a special singing and was baptized two weeks later. That was the beginning of my walk with the Lord.

I learned that God loved me and that I can always trust in His care. We had weekly prayer meetings in our home where I prayed to the Lord about everything. I understood early on that God hears and answers our prayers. Later, as I experienced the hardships of my life, these spiritual truths often brought me comfort and strength. They were promises on which I could always depend, no matter how difficult the days ahead became.

My mother and father in 1943, holding their last toddler, me

My sisters, left to right: Betty, Mary Jo, Rose, Imojean, Addie Kay, and myself

My brothers, left to right: Ralph, Roy, Russell, and Sam

My brother, R. A. (Robert Alexander) who passed away at the age of 47

CHAPTER TWO:

SCHOOL YEARS/FAMILY TRANSITIONS

My school years began at Clifton Hills Grammar School. Later I went to East Lake Grammar School, East Lake Junior High School, and finally, Kirkman High School. Because all my friends had both a mom and a dad at home, I remember feeling insecure around them. I could not relate to the other girls as they talked about their dads and the fun things they did together.

My clothing was also a source of embarrassment to me. We were pinching our pennies very tightly at home, so new clothes were not in our budget. I wore a lot of hand-me-downs from my older sisters, while my friends seemed to have nicer clothes. Even so, I was generally happy and grateful for what Mama could provide as a single parent.

My days in the classrooms were pleasant, and I loved my teachers. Being in the junior high school chorus was the highlight for me. The music and singing always made me feel better. My favorite area of study was business. I was encouraged to take many business courses and to consider paralegal work as a career. My school days are enjoyable memories, and many of my school friends are still special people in my life.

Things were going smoothly for our family for about three years after we moved to Chattanooga.

As my older siblings finished high school and began working, they also became independent or married and moved away from our home. My oldest sister, Betty, and her friend moved to Anchorage, Alaska, to work. She later got married and was not available to help us anymore. Mary Jo married John and moved to California. A year later Rose married Chris, and they moved to California, too.

That left only my two older sisters, my brother, and me to help Mama at home. A short time later, my sisters quit school and went to work to bring in more income for us. Before long, Imojean and Earl married and moved to Florida. Shortly after that, Addie Kay and Kenneth married and left for California.

At this point, Marion and I were the only siblings left at home. Marion got a job at Goodlet's grocery store, and I started babysitting to help meet our family expenses. Before he was able to graduate, Marion quit school and began working full time. Two years later he married Wilma and moved to California to be near the rest of the family out there.

Even though I was willing to work more and bring in additional income for us, my mother did not want me to work full-time. I always thought this was because she just did not want her "baby" to grow up, become independent, and leave her like all the others had done. She made it clear, however, that it was important to her that I graduate from high school.

The reality that some women are abused had not been a part of my world. My brothers, brothers-in-law, and even my dad (from the stories I heard about him) were all good, kind, faithful men. I was seventeen before I realized that some men purposely and intentionally hurt women.

A Glimmer of Hope

CHAPTER THREE:

MY FIRST MARRIAGE

At the age of seventeen, I met Mack at school. Besides being a classmate, he was also a "sack boy" at Goodlet's grocery store. My sister, Imojean, worked there with him and thought he would be a good person for me to date. On our first date in September 1958, he drove us in his 1947 Chevy to a drive-in movie starring Humphrey Bogart. Later, he taught me how to drive that car. He was always particularly good to me. He was polite and never used offensive language. His mom was nice and treated me like a daughter. When I was a high school senior, she helped me get a part-time job at Effron Department Store. I was finally able to convince Mama that the extra money would help us pay the bills.

Before too long, I noticed that Mack started getting jealous of me spending time with my friends. One time my friend and I were standing outside talking to her boyfriend. Mack came up and, without warning, slapped me across my face. He said he had better not catch me talking to another guy again. I was shocked. When Imojean heard what had happened she told him that if he ever slapped me again, she would knock his head off. He apologized and did not become violent again until after we were married. I wish I had known then that I had just experienced abusive behavior. *Purposely hurting another person by slapping them is an abusive behavior.* That was my first red flag of possible trouble ahead, which I ignored and simply hoped for the best. I had no idea that the long-term consequence of continuing that type of relationship with Mack would be a marriage that included both physical and verbal abuse.

We became engaged in our senior year and were married on February 12, 1959. We lived with Mama for about two months until we both graduated from Kirkman High School in May of 1959.

Mack and I moved into a single bedroom apartment in a large house on Rossville Boulevard. Mack worked full time at a box factory, and with his income we were able to buy some furniture for our little apartment. I was already pregnant with our first baby. Shortly after we were on our own, the second red flag of trouble started waving wildly.

Mack was often irritated and angry when he came home from work, and he began taking his temper out on me. I tried my best to prepare a good meal for him, but if it did not meet his approval, he would throw the food on the floor, yell at me to clean up the mess, and then punch me with his fist until I had everything cleaned again. Often, he would pick up the entire table and dump everything on the floor. Many weeks, there were more meals dumped than eaten. I was horrified that he would dare do these things, but I was too embarrassed and humiliated to tell Mama or my sisters.

I was young, naïve, poor, and scared to death. He had me trapped, and I felt like I had no one to help me out of this horrible situation. I left him many times in my mind but could not bring myself to physically walk out that apartment door. He threatened that if I ever tried to leave him, he would kill me and cut me up in so many pieces that no one could ever find me. I often wondered how I ever thought I loved this man or even believed his claims that he loved me.

Mack's intolerable outbursts escalated from supper time drama to him slugging and punching me for just about any reason. When I was seven months pregnant with our baby, he pushed me so hard that I fell down the steps in our apartment. The lady who lived downstairs called an ambulance, and I was taken to the hospital. The baby was alright, but I was very bruised. The police questioned me, but I was too afraid to say that Mack had pushed me down the steps. I was heartbroken and totally stressed by the whole situation. Mack just could not handle all the tears. He told me he was sorry and that he would not hurt me again.

Mack kept his word for several months, and I thanked God for the peaceful time. I could see a glimmer of hope that he had changed, and I hoped we would have better days ahead, especially with our baby soon to be born.

A Glimmer of Hope

CHAPTER FOUR:

OUR BABIES

Our baby girl (Elaine) was born in September 1959. For about four months, Mack seemed to be happy with being a father and was being much kinder toward me. It seemed like he had really changed. We moved in January 1960 to a different apartment at East Lake Park.

The next month, I discovered I was pregnant again. Mack's behavior completely changed when I told him another baby was on the way. He became outraged and accused me of having been with another man. He yelled that this baby was not his, and he punched me with his fist over and over.

He never eased up on his meanness during the entire pregnancy. I was totally exhausted and felt defeated, but I held on to the hope that I would see that same positive change in Mack that I had seen after Elaine was born. Our second child was born in October 1960. We named him McKinley. Elaine was just thirteen months old. We now had two babies under the age of two.

Mack did not soften up a bit after McKinley was born. In fact, he had no desire to hold his little son or to even feed him. Things got much worse after McKinley developed colic and was crying all the time. Once when he was four weeks old, I left McKinley asleep with Mack while I took Elaine to the store with me. When I came back, I opened the door and immediately heard my baby screaming. I ran into the bedroom and saw Mack shaking his bed so hard that McKinley was rolling all over the mattress and was screaming his lungs out.

I told Mack I would never leave him alone with the baby again. That was a promise I kept, too. I tried to protect McKinley from his father after that, but our son feared his daddy. Mack always paid more attention to Elaine than he did to McKinley. I once mentioned his favoritism toward Elaine to Mack. He punched me again and again, yelling that our son was not his child. It seemed that Mack never would accept McKinley as his own child.

CHAPTER FIVE:

LEAVING THE FIRST TIME

Mama asked me once during a visit why I had on such heavy make-up. When she wiped some of it off, she saw the bruises and busted lip under the make-up. I had not told anyone about the beatings. It was just too humiliating. I could not hide the black eyes and other injuries from Mama or my sisters any longer. They were very upset and concerned about me and my babies. They encouraged me to leave Mack and get out of my situation.

After a particularly bad pounding, I knew in my heart I had to get out of there and leave Mack. I took the children and stayed for a few weeks with my mom, who had moved back to Gadsden, Alabama.

Mack knew we probably were at Mama's and came down to her house. He seemed terribly sorry and said he would never hurt me again. He said things would be better, and again, I held on to that glimmer of hope that he had really changed. He was very sincere, and I believed that things could be better this time. I decided we should go back home and try again.

There were many good changes, and Mack seemed to follow through on his promise to change. There were no more angry outbursts or insufferable beatings, no more food on the floor, no more kicks or punches, and no more insulting, foul-mouthed tirades. Mack even paid a little more attention to the children.

When Mack's parents purchased a second home, they offered to let us to live in their previous three-bedroom home on 15th Avenue in East Lake for just $250 a month. It was a cute little house with a yard for the children and plenty of room for all of us. I really looked forward to living there. The bright, sunny dream of my happy future encouraged me after the horrible beginning of our marriage.

Once we moved into his parent's house however, those sunny dreams became horrible nightmares. Mack again became unbearable toward me with his verbal haranguing and physical violence. He picked at everything he thought I was doing wrong, especially cooking, cleaning, and caring for the children. When he started picking, I knew a beating was coming next.

As if all that was not enough, I had to tell Mack that I was pregnant yet again. He was infuriated about having another baby and so was his mother. She got angry and said it was not good for Mack to have such a burden on his shoulders. She believed he would quit punching me once he "grew up." His Daddy never said a word about what Mack was doing to me. Ever.

Our third child, a daughter we named Eunice, was born November 17, 1962. Mack seemed to calm down once she was born. He was a good Daddy to her and paid attention to her. But some things did not change. Mack still was not treating McKinley well. He also continued to attack me whenever he became infuriated by the slightest of triggers. Sometimes he said he was sorry for the way he treated me, but that did not stop his meanness from happening again.

In 1963, Elaine started kindergarten at East Lake Baptist Church. I started working at Goodlet's grocery store full time. Mack's parents decided to sell their house that we were living in, so we had to move again. By the summer of 1964, we were living in a house in Fort Oglethorpe, Georgia. Once we made the move, Mack seemed to calm down again, and life was becoming more even keeled.

In the fall, McKinley started kindergarten. He had trouble at school right away. He stuttered and could not talk plainly. The other little boys would make fun of him and gang up on him. Mack did not try to help McKinley with these problems. Instead, he would call his son a sissy, scream at him, shake him, and try to make him fight back. Mack did not like for McKinley to get any extra help with his speech at school. He simply thought McKinley would outgrow the stuttering. However, the teacher said that was not true.

McKinley's teacher started helping him with his speech, and later in first grade he received special help with speech classes at the Speech and Hearing Center in downtown Chattanooga. Mack did not want to pay for McKinley's speech classes and got quite angry at me for taking him there for two years. The principal at the grammar school helped with the teasing boys and helped get McKinley into football. Life at home quieted down again, and we all felt a great relief. That little glimmer of hope started glowing in my heart once more. Maybe Mack had finally calmed down for good this time.

A Glimmer of Hope

CHAPTER SIX:

LEAVING THE SECOND TIME

Most years we took our family vacation to Daytona Beach, Florida, in August before the kids started back to school. That sounds like a good thing, but for us it was horrible. Every year, it was the same. As soon as we started packing the suitcases, Mack would get irritated about the way we were folding our clothes or about what we were packing. I could always expect that he would get physical toward me either before we left the house or certainly, by the time we got to the hotel in Florida. It was like that every year.

When we would start back home, he would get unbearable, even with the kids nearby. Once, on the way home from Florida, he knocked my head against the car window. The kids cried and told him to quit pounding me. He stopped at that point, but the least little irritation would set him off again.

When the kids were teens, we went on a two-week vacation out west. Everything went well until the last two days. Mack told me that he wanted to get rid of me. I told the kids to stay near me because their dad was going to pick a fight with me. McKinley heard him starting to harangue me. He very bravely told his Daddy that if he hurt me in any way, the police would be called, and they would put him in jail. Mack cooled down for the time being, but on our way home he began fussing again. I said not one word to him, and the kids kept quiet. We got home without any commotion, but the next day everything broke loose. Mack was so infuriated that he broke my nose in two places. I decided right then that I needed to leave.

I took the children and stayed with my sister in Tampa, Florida, for a week. After talking with my sister, I decided we needed to move in with my niece in Chattanooga so the children could start the school year there. Mack found us though and said he wanted us to return to the house. He again promised to never hurt me. We stayed with my niece one more week while I considered my options. Once we returned home Mack controlled his anger for only about six months. Every time I moved back in with Mack, I was hopeful that he would finally change for good.

CHAPTER SEVEN:

TROUBLE AHEAD

I was ever the optimist, but that optimism did not last long. We would have peace and quiet at home for a few months before we had another knock-down drag-out episode. Mack would revert to all his old behaviors, except by this time he was completely intolerable.

He started beating me every day. When he came home, he fussed about the least little thing and whacked me because of it. He went back to turning the table over with our dinner on it. He knocked me to the floor and kicked me in the stomach with his heel. He yelled that I had better clean it up and punched me until it was all clean.

The children were becoming terrorized by what they were seeing and hearing. It was during that time when I began to feed the children early and get them to their rooms before Mack even got home.

Once, when I was 29 years old (1970), Mack knocked and pushed me around in our bedroom. He knocked me onto the bed, and my foot got caught in the railing along the side. The pain was excruciating. Mack drove me to the hospital, and McKinley came with us. Once there, Mack refused to go inside. He made McKinley go in with me to the emergency room, but before we left, he told us we had better keep our mouths shut about what happened or he would kill us all. The x-rays at the hospital showed that four toes on my right foot were broken from the fall. When asked what happened, I told the doctor the truth, but said I did not want the police involved.

The police came anyway and talked to us at the hospital. Later they came to the house and talked to Mack. They did not take him to jail because I did not press charges against him. After they left, Mack just said, "You better be thankful you didn't press charges against me, or else I would have killed you!" But he did not lay a hand on me that time. Due to that injury, I could not work for about three weeks.

CHAPTER EIGHT:

THE AFFAIR

While I was busy working at Goodlet's, some friends informed me that Mack had been having an affair for the past two years with another employee at the store. I had no idea this was happening and was totally blindsided. Mack had taken our young children with him when he visited his girlfriend. To keep them from telling me, Mack threatened that he would kill them and me if they ever told. The children now feared him, not only because of all his outbursts of anger that they had observed at home, but also because he had involved them in his affair and had threatened them with harm.

I really could not imagine any woman having an affair with a man like Mack. He surely treated them much better while he was seeing them on the side than he treated me as his wife. He was like two people in one body. A perfect gentleman when in public, but a mean, despicable man in private.

One night after I had learned about the affair, Mack pounded me so violently on my face that I could hardly see. My vision was very blurry, and I felt like my whole face had been smashed. I decided right then and there that I was leaving and taking the children with me.

I knew Mack would have a total tirade when I told him that I already knew about his girlfriend and that I was leaving, so I decided to tell him about it the next day at the safest place I knew. Mack was working at Goodlet's grocery store in Tiftonia. I knew I would be protected by his manager and the many workers there.

In the morning, I put on heavy make-up to conceal the black and blue bruises. Mack's manager called him back into a back office where I confronted him with my news. I was scared to death, but I knew I was safe for the time being. Besides telling Mack that I knew about his girlfriend and that I was leaving him and taking the children, I also told him in no uncertain terms not to come back to the house while I was packing. I did not tell him where I was going, even though I already had a plan.

I went back to the house and packed enough clothes for an extended stay out of town. I then went by the school and picked up the children who were now in the third, fifth, and sixth grades. I told the children that I was taking them someplace where we would all be safe. They were worried that Mack might think that they had told me about the girlfriend and about his threats to kill us all, and they were worried that Mack would come after us.

We went to live with Betty, my friend in Huntsville, Alabama, for about two and a half months while my face and body healed. Before long I looked better and felt better. The children were happy and attending school in Huntsville. After a while I knew I needed to get back to work at Goodlet's in Rossville for an income to support my children.

I also wanted the children to get settled into a place of our own. I had to find an inexpensive place where Mack could not find us. He had not made any contact with us while we were at Betty's, so I was sure he did not really know where we were. I also had heard that his affair was over when her husband found out about it.

A Glimmer of Hope

CHAPTER NINE:

THE KIDNAPPING

We moved back to Georgia and rented a furnished trailer in Chickamauga. Everything was fine for about three weeks. The children were back at their school in Ft. Oglethorpe. My friend, Linda, volunteered to pick up the children from school. They stayed at her house until I could pick them up after work. I told the school administration that no one was to pick up the children except for me or my friend, Linda. Certainly, their father was NOT to pick them up!

We were all happy in the trailer and felt safe in the small trailer park. I took various routes back and forth to and from work just in case Mack decided to follow me after work. Fortunately, I never once saw him trailing me at all.

One day I got a call at work that scared me to death. It was Mack. He had the children, and he threatened that he would only let me have them if I met him at the graveyard near our trailer in Chickamauga.

My heart was throbbing. I left immediately and headed for the graveyard. I was scared to death as to what he was going to do to me and the children. He was already there when I arrived. I got out of my car to go get the children. I told them to get out and get in my car so we could go home and have supper.

But Mack said, "Oh, no! You are not going to get the kids! And you're never going to see them again!"

Then he zoomed off with them. They were crying and screaming for me. I tried to follow him, but he was already too far ahead. I was hysterical and beside myself. Where was he going? What was he going to do with the children?

I went by Mack's house, but they were not there. I went by work and told my supervisor. He sent someone from their security department to see if they could be located. I went back to the trailer and prayed with all my might that the Lord would keep my children safe.

In the morning, I contacted the school to see how Mack had taken the children. The principal was very upset that the children had been mistakenly released to Mack by a substitute who did not follow the proper procedures. Within a few days, the security agent found Mack, who confessed that he had taken the children to his aunt's house in Knoxville and had left them there. Mack claimed he could do that because they were his children, too.

When the children were finally able to return to the trailer, they were very distraught by what had happened to them. Mack said that he was sorry that he had taken the children and had upset them so much. He apologized for all the other horrible things he had done when we lived with him. He promised that if the children and I moved back to the house with him, he would never hurt me or run around on me again.

After so many earlier broken promises, I really did not believe him anymore. I was also convinced that, if we lived separately, Mack would continue to grab the children away from me whenever he could.

I finally decided to try once more, so we moved back into Mack's house in Ft. Oglethorpe. Things settled down again. Mack even started going to Clifton Hills Baptist Church with us and his mom on Sundays. We were all happy about the positive changes that were happening in our family. That little glimmer of hope began to shine brightly in my heart again as I was sure Mack had really changed this time.

A Glimmer of Hope

CHAPTER TEN:

LEAVING THE FOURTH TIME

About six months later, I noticed the old Mack coming back into the picture. He came home later and later from work. He started picking fights with me about the kids, his clothes, or his food. When he started hitting me again and calling me horrible names, I knew our peaceful time was over. I tried to talk things out with him, and sometimes he would say he was sorry.

Then I realized what was really happening. Mack was running around on me again. I knew instinctively that he was seeing someone else by the unusual things he started to do. He insisted that I give him my payday checks. From that, he only gave me three or four dollars a week. He filled up my car with gas and went with me to the store to buy groceries. He always had to know where I was. He started something with me every day so he could use his fist and batter me for whatever had made him angry.

One day I found out the details about what I had suspected. Mack had a new girlfriend who he was meeting during his lunch hour at a motel in the Lookout Mountain area. I was so mad and really hated Mack for the way he had treated me and always accused me of having a boyfriend.

I was completely incensed. Right then I drove to the motel and saw his car parked outside a room on the main floor. I knocked on the door. Mack opened the door and before he could say a word, I told him his clothes would be on the front porch. I told him in no uncertain terms to stay away from the house and do not come in again. I told him if he came home, I would call the police and have him put in jail. Later that day he came and picked up his clothes from the porch, but did not knock or try to come in.

The next day when I got home from work, I saw his car in the driveway and knew Mack was inside the house. When I entered the living room, Mack came storming in from the bedroom. He was boiling mad. I was scared to death. He slugged me so badly in the face over and over. My eyes were black and blue, my lips were busted, and my nose had been broken in two places. One last punch and one last name-calling, and then he slammed the door as he left.

On his way out he told me he would be moving back in, like it or not. That night I moved my things into the children's room and slept with them. The next day Mack was back and stayed alone in our bedroom from that point on. I doctored myself the best that I could, but I still could not go to work for about two weeks.

Two of my coworkers at the grocery store knew something was wrong when I kept calling in sick. They came by the house and saw my condition. I was in such bad shape that I scared them. They insisted that I get out of my situation and wanted me to go with them. I promised I would leave Mack.

I did not tell them I already had a plan in mind for leaving.

Later that week I took the children, and we moved in with my niece, Jane. We stayed there for about three weeks. I contacted a lawyer and started the process of getting a divorce.

In the meantime, Mack snatched the kids from school. He called me at Jane's and threatened that if I did not come back to him, I would never see the kids again.

The kids were crying and saying, "Please, Mom, come back. We are scared."

Mack promised, once more, that he would change, and I, once more, decided to try yet again. I called the lawyer and canceled the divorce process. Of course, Mack's promises were not ever kept for more than a few months.

A Glimmer of Hope

CHAPTER ELEVEN:

HOSPITAL STAYS

In March 1974 I was in the hospital for eight days. I had to have my gallbladder and part of my colon removed. When I came home, Mack helped take care of me for the first week. After that short period, he resumed his meanness. He pushed me, knocked me down, and punched me in my stomach. I had to go back in the hospital for five more days because my stomach was bleeding.

The day I got back home, Mack stayed out until late that night and was full of meanness and hatefulness when he returned. He tried to slug me, but this time I told him if he hit me, I would call the police on him. He decided to go to the bedroom and refused to talk at all.

I had to be off work for six weeks from the gallbladder surgery. Rather than being restful and relaxing, life at home was worse than ever. Mack went back to turning over the table full of food and picking fights about anything and everything.

I tried to stay quiet and keep the children out of his way. I tried to do everything the way that he wanted it. But nothing helped. As soon as the children were out of the house, he pounded me and assaulted me all over my body. I could not wait to get out of the house and back to work.

Later that summer, I started helping Mack's mother on the weekends to clean and do whatever she needed since she had been diagnosed with cancer. While I took care of her, Mack did nothing to help. Near the end of her life, she began to bleed out of her mouth and nose and had to go to the hospital. I stayed day and night with her. Even during this time, Mack picked fights with me. He gave me a black eye and busted my mouth three different times while his mom was in the hospital. I kept going to help her until the day she died in 1974.

After her death, we needed to pick out her casket and her clothes for the funeral. Mack insisted he had to wear a suit for this trip to the funeral home. Just because I did not have his suit ready for him to wear that day, he smacked me so hard that my lips turned wrong side out, and my eyes were black and blue. People noticed how bad I looked at his mother's funeral. No one could believe he would be so vicious toward me, but he did not care that people thought his behavior was shocking, nor that he was terrorizing me.

About a year after Mack's mom died, his dad had to have surgery. I went to his house to fix his food and do general cleaning while he was recuperating. Once again, Mack did not help at all. He continued to show his ugly attitude and hateful anger. Once his dad got better, I quit going over there. I told Mack he could help his dad from then on because I would not be doing it anymore. I got a black eye for saying that but, at that point, I did not care what he did.

CHAPTER TWELVE:

THE BEGINNING OF THE END

I worked at Goodlet's grocery store as a cashier for fourteen years from 1963-1977, and after that I worked in the lab at Erlanger Hospital. Through all those working years, Mack started his harassment on me nearly every morning. I often went to work with black eyes or a busted mouth. Heavy make-up helped to hide my many bruises. Beyond the bruises and busted lips, I suffered the pain of a broken nose twice, broken toes, and broken ribs. I lost weeks of work due to recuperation from my injuries. My co-workers and supervisors were concerned about my safety and urged me to leave Mack. It was constantly on my mind to do just that.

I found enough courage to leave Mack about nine times through the years, but every time he convinced me to come back. He could be very persuasive and earnest when he wanted me to come back home. I always hoped and thought things would be better. I finally had to admit to myself that Mack did not know how to love someone else. He never told the kids that he loved them or uttered those words to me either. Rather, he expended his energy on chasing other women and being hateful toward his family.

I stayed with Mack because of my children. I worried constantly about them. They needed their own home, clothing, food, etc. I knew I could not keep yanking them away to stay with relatives or friends whenever Mack exploded at home. Yet, I could not afford a place of my own.

Fortunately, the children very seldom were the objects of his violence, but they were a witness to it. They were always afraid he would lash out at them like he did to me. There were times that Mack was more civil, and we all just relaxed a little. We measured those times by the months, sometimes as much as six months. But just as things began to feel normal, Mack would suddenly begin to terrorize us again.

Over time I reached the point to where I did not care about myself anymore or about the beatings I endured. I was exhausted and defeated. Emotionally I felt numb. I just prayed that I could get the kids through high school and on their own.

All my personal dreams and desires died, and the glimmer of hope within me became the tiniest flicker. My goals were only to keep on going to work, taking care of my children's needs, and keeping our house in decent condition. I could only deal with one day at a time. At times I let my mind pretend that I was somewhere else with the kids. I dreamed about being in California with my sisters or being in Alabama with Mama.

Each year that I lived with Mack, I feared him more and more, knowing that if I did not have everything perfectly right with his food or if the house/ clothes were not immaculate, I faced another beating or terrible assault. I began to believe that I must deserve all the whippings.

When the kids reached their teenage years, Mack became even worse. He slapped me nearly every day when I came in from work. He stomped on me, threatened me by pointing a gun at me, and jabbed me with our kitchen knives. I would get hysterical and start crying. Finally, he would stop.

One Saturday my teen-agers were out on dates. Mack had to work late, or so he said. He came home while I was ironing clothes. He started fussing with me over nothing. He punched me so forcefully that he cracked two of my ribs. It took me five weeks to heal from this hateful attack.

When McKinley was seventeen, he was out on a date. Mack came home from work already mad. He started cussing at me for cooking pork-chops. He dumped all the food on the floor. He started slugging me until I fell. He had me on the floor and was kicking me both in my stomach and on my sides. Then he pulled a gun on me and pointed it to my head. I really thought that was the end for me.

But it so happened that McKinley came in and saw me on the floor with his dad holding a gun to my head. He ran out of the house, ran to Bob and Lorraine's house across the street, and called the police. The police came to the house and took Mack to jail, but Mack's dad bailed him out. Mack spent that night with his parents.

I left the next day with the kids and went to my mom's place in Alabama. After two weeks I came back because the kids needed to be in school, and I needed to be back at my job.

Mack said he would not ever threaten me with a gun or knife again. His dad took the gun away. Of course, I trusted his word that he would control his anger toward me. Peace at home lasted for about a month. Then he started smacking me again nearly every day. I realized then that he would never, ever change for good.

I made up my mind that I would just take care of the kids and go to work. I no longer cared about trying to please Mack anymore. I filed for divorce for the second time. I was finally ready to leave and take the kids with me.

However, since the kids were in high school, they did not want to move and leave their friends. Elaine and McKinley were so close to graduating from Lakeview High School. Instead, they confronted Mack with the threat to leave him and never see him again if he dared to batter me again. As always, Mack promised that he would never hurt me again.

So, crazy me, I canceled the divorce process and stayed at home with Mack. That was the worst thing I could have done. His promise was good for only about seven months.

CHAPTER THIRTEEN:

THE DIVORCE

Once all the children had grown up and moved out of the house, I was left at home by myself with Mack. One night his brother and two of his friends came over to work on his brother's show car. Mack demanded that I fix supper for everyone. After I had cooked a good meal, Mack cussed me out in front of them. He accused me of being a sloppy cook and a tramp. The men were embarrassed at his behavior. They told me the food was good and that they appreciated the dinner. When they left, Mack started slugging and punching me again.

I got to the point where I hated Mack. Every time I came home from work, it was a fight. He whipped me more and kept threatening to cut me up in pieces so nobody could ever find me. I hated him so much, I could not stand to be in the same room with him. I told him I would leave him and never come back. Any glimmer of hope that I had for our marriage had now been snuffed out by Mack's continual meanness, beatings, and running around on me. Yet, when I threatened to leave, Mack always started acting better for a little while.

At one point, Eunice moved back in with us after her divorce. She was pregnant at that time. Mack was acting better until Eunice had her baby. I worked first shift, and Eunice worked second shift, so I kept the baby for her while she worked.

During that time, I found out that Mack was running around on me once again for the third time. I told Eunice I was going to leave Mack and move out. She found herself an apartment and was in the process of moving when she discovered she was pregnant yet again. Mack found out about it and went off the deep end. He was furious that she was pregnant again so soon after her first baby was born.

There was a huge argument. He shoved and knocked her so hard that she flipped over a chair. I told him I would call the police if he did not stop. I picked up the baby and left. I told him I hoped Eunice would kill him. When I came back to the house later, he was there, but Eunice was gone. Mack was his typical hateful self and smacked me severely.

Eunice was terrified of Mack's rantings and ravings, so she moved as soon as she could into the Battlewood Apartments. One day in 1985 she called me to come over because her second baby was sick, and she needed some help. Mack went with me. He started fussing with Eunice. He got very mad at her, so I said that we needed to leave.

I started out the door with Mack behind me. Before I knew what happened, he knocked me down a flight of steel steps. The fall cracked my tailbone and cracked my pelvis. I had to stay in bed for two weeks. The police picked him up, but his dad got him out on bail again. I was not able to go back to work for four weeks.

I knew I had to leave Mack for good. One morning when Erlanger called me in to work at 2:00 a.m., I got up to go to work. I was in the bathroom fixing my face and hair. Mack came in saying that I was going to see my boyfriend. He shoved me and knocked me into the bathtub, constantly pounding on me and kicking me. I do not know how I crawled out of the house, but I got to the car. He hollered for me to get back inside the house, but I told him I would never come back to the house again. I never did go back. I hated him so much.

I left Mack for good in 1987. Once he realized I was gone and not about to return, he was infuriated. He tried pushing me off the freeway with his van. He came in Erlanger Hospital and put black roses on the door where I worked. He tried to grab me from my job.

I never went anywhere by myself. He threatened to kill me many times before our divorce. He desperately wanted me to come back to him. He had lost his verbal and physical punching bag, and he could not stand it. He begged and cried. He promised he would change and would never hurt me again. But I knew he would never change.

If I had gone back to him, he would have eventually killed me. The divorce was final in 1988.

A Glimmer of Hope

CHAPTER FOURTEEN:

MY SECOND MARRIAGE

Once I left Mack and was divorced, my life total-ly changed for the good. My niece told an old friend, Eugene, that I was in the process of getting a divorce. He called me and asked me to go out to dinner with him. We went out a few times and went to some car races together.

I had known Eugene and his ex-wife for about five years. I first met him when he was the coach of McKinley's elementary little league football team. Eugene had owned his own mechanic shop on 35th Street for many years, and sometimes we had taken our cars there for him to service. So, we were famil-iar with each other, but came to love each other once we started dating. It was not long before we became engaged.

Once my divorce from Mack was final, Eugene and I got married on March 18, 1988, at the Wood-more Church of God. I moved into his house, and we were happy together. He was so good to me. There were never any threats, beatings, or name-callings. He was tender and kind toward me, and I loved be-ing loved and treated like a valuable partner. I loved cooking for him and keeping the house in order. We even redid his house together. We traveled out of town a lot. We just loved being with each other.

We were happy for about five and a half years.

In October of 1993 Eugene started acting differently toward me. He changed the way he was acting at home. He did not want to stay home much and seemed to be gone a lot. He started working late.

One afternoon Eugene came in the house and told me he did not love me anymore. He wanted me to move out of the house. I was shocked and hurt. I had trusted Eugene and had felt secure in our marriage. I had put a lot of work and money into the house and felt deeply that was where I belonged.

I did not want a divorce, but Eugene wanted me to get the divorce, and let him be free. Then I found out he was involved with an old girlfriend. My sister and her husband who were in town from California and my brother helped me move into an apartment. I went through my second divorce.

CHAPTER FIFTEEN:

MARRIED AGAIN

Eugene had a serious stroke just a few months later in 1993 while he was at his girlfriend's house. Eugene's daughter-in-law called to tell me he had had the stroke and that he was at Erlanger Hospital, where I was working in the lab. One of my peers at Erlanger told me that a woman was in his room and sitting on his bed. I just knew that woman was the girlfriend Eugene had been seeing. I went up to his room, but she had already left. His brother and sister-in-law were there with him instead.

I told Eugene that if I could help him in any way, just let me know. Eugene spent a while in the hospital and then went through rehab. Once he got back on his feet and was able to go home, his girlfriend left town. I guess she was not interested in being his care-taker at home.

Six months later Eugene called me and wanted to see me, but I refused. He called and called. I refused and refused. He called my sister and my brother-in-law in California. He begged them to talk me into coming back to him. I kept the refusal wall up for about eight months. In the end, I finally gave up and agreed to talk to him. He said that all he wanted was just to talk to me. So, he came over to my apartment, and we started talking.

Before long we started seeing each other again. We had been going together for about two months when he asked me to marry him again. I agreed, and we began to make plans to remarry on the same date that we had been married seven years earlier.

We remarried on March 18, 1995. We were happy again, and he was so kind to me. We started going to Delray Baptist Church, where we had a lot of friends. Everything was good again.

In 2004 Eugene started having a lot of health issues with his diabetes, his kidneys, and the platelets in his blood. Finally, Eugene had a heart attack and had to have open heart surgery. It was a terrible year with no breaks from all the health problems. Eugene had to give up his shop on 35th Street. He gave the business to his son, who later lost the whole thing.

After he fully recuperated from his heart attack, Eugene had a great longing to have a shop again. His equity from the 35th Street shop was gone, so he wanted me to use my retirement money to open Ashland Terrace Collision Center. So, I did, and we opened that business together. Everything went well until Eugene developed serious problems with his feet because of diabetes. One day the doctors discovered gangrene in his foot, and his leg had to be amputated at the knee.

After that Eugene changed. He blamed me and his brother for his leg amputation. He got so bitter and hateful about his leg that he would not even try to walk with his artificial leg. He just stayed in his wheelchair and was angry all the time. He was very mean to me with his mouth, saying things I never thought would come out of his mouth. I realized then that abuse happens in many ways and for different reasons.

I tried to take good care of Eugene. I got him a good doctor and hospital care. I prayed all the time, asking God to be with him and to help me keep my mind straight. I prayed that God would change Eugene's heart and attitude. I hoped his family knew I tried to do everything possible for him. I know God saw all my efforts.

Eugene continued to get worse about everything. He did not want to go to church anymore. I told him I was going to go because God helps us in our times of trouble, and we can get help from the Lord through the services at church. This went on for about three years. He did not want to do anything. He just wanted to stay home and go to the shop. He did not want me to be at the shop at all.

Eugene's health turned even worse in 2009. His kidneys started failing. He could not get dialysis because his heart was too bad. By March Eugene was in MICU at Memorial Hospital due to his kidneys and heart.

He told me during that time some shocking news. He said that I would lose everything that I had when he died. I could not believe what he was saying. I thought he was kidding me. He was not. He was telling me the truth.

When Eugene was released from the hospital under hospice care, I found out the IRS was closing the shop down because Eugene had not paid the taxes for a full year. I asked Eugene why he did that to me. All he did was laugh and did not offer any explanation. Eugene died the next week in April 2009.

CHAPTER SIXTEEN:

WIDOWHOOD

My life was turned completely upside down after Eugene passed away. I asked God to help me because I had no idea how to handle everything. I tried to keep the shop open, but some of the employees began doing jobs on the side and kept the income for themselves. I tried to keep the wrecker service open by selling everything I could to pay all the bills. At every turn I kept finding more and more unopened or unpaid bills at both the shop and at home.

In the end, I lost both the business and the buildings. I had to get a lawyer and file a Chapter 13 bankruptcy. The bank repossessed everything we had on loan. The IRS took the house to pay tax bills. Eugene left me in an extreme financial mess. Through it all, though, I had faith that God would take care of me and lead me to a better day.

Since I had no house or place to live, I went to California for fourteen months to live with my sister. It was a good time for me to think things through and decide what to do next. I missed my children and grandchildren. I missed my church, Delray Baptist Church. I loved the pastor, Ronnie, and his wife, Carol, who always helped me a lot with my spiritual needs. Brother Ronnie told me he hoped I did not get bitter over losing everything. He told me to always look up and never look down. He said to read Psalm 4 often.

I have tried to remember these verses every day.

Psalm 4   *"Hear me when I call, O God of my righteousness: thou hast enlarged me when I was in distress; have mercy upon me and hear my prayer.*

2 O ye sons of men, how long will ye turn my glory into shame? how long will ye love vanity, and seek after leasing? Selah.

3 But know that the Lord hath set apart him that is godly for himself: the Lord will hear when I call unto him.

4 Stand in awe, and sin not: commune with your own heart upon your bed and be still. Selah.

5 Offer the sacrifices of righteousness and put your trust in the Lord.

6 There be many that say, who will shew us any good? Lord, lift thou up the light of thy countenance upon us.

7 Thou hast put gladness in my heart, more than in the time that their corn and their wine increased.

8 I will both lay me down in peace, and sleep: for thou, Lord, only make me dwell in safety."

When I felt I was ready to start over, I moved back to Georgia. I asked God to help me find an apartment that I could afford. He helped me get one in Charleston, TN, close to my son and daughter-in-law. I stayed there about eight months, coming down to the Chattanooga area on weekends to see my daughters and friends, and to attend my church. Then I decided to live with my daughter in Ringgold,

Georgia, where I would be closer to my doctors and church.

During this time, the IRS was still taking almost all my money each month. I kept trying to negotiate a smaller monthly payment plan, but the IRS would not consider that at all. After many calls to the IRS, a helpful lady at the Atlanta office was assigned to my case. Eight long years later, we were finally able to work out a settlement, and my case was closed.

A Glimmer of Hope

CHAPTER SEVENTEEN:

FINAL THOUGHTS

Abuse is seldom a topic of daily conversation unless it is being experienced personally or by someone you care about. Unfortunately, I lived in a physically and verbally abusive relationship for twenty-eight years with Mack and experienced verbal abuse from Eugene for five years.

I wish with all my heart that I had left Mack when my children were small, but I was petrified that he would hurt me and the kids. Many people told me to leave Mack, and they could not understand why I did not pack my bags and take the children away from him.

Believe me, I wondered that myself many times, but of course, it is so much easier to say than to do. I wish I had known about the dangers and heartbreaks that living with an abuser would bring into my life. I had no idea. I was in no way prepared for those years of abuse.

I am not a counselor or professional advisor. However, I have learned many lessons along the way which I hope to pass on to my younger family members and to friends who are experiencing any forms of abuse. Retelling my story has been intensely heartbreaking for me. I hate the details and wish I could forget all of them. However, I have shared my story in the hopes that I can help others to be able to avoid difficult or even horrible times in life at the hands of an abuser, as well as the frequent aftereffects from abuse of depression, anxiety, and PTSD. I hope you can learn these lessons from my experience, and that you will not have to experience abuse yourself.

LESSON ONE:
Do everything you can to avoid becoming involved with an abusive person.

Abusive individuals and their victims come from every race, age, income, culture, gender, profession, and religion. According to the Center for Disease Control and Prevention, one in three women has experienced partner violence. People with abusive tendencies can seem very normal, charming, attentive, and attractive at first. If your background is as stable and loving as mine was, you might not even be aware that there are individuals who will purposely and intentionally hurt you. Some types of abuse are:

Physical abuse is what I experienced from Mack. This happens when a person purposely and intentionally causes pain, injury, or trauma to another by bodily contact. It is done on purpose, not accidentally. Common examples are striking, kicking, biting, burning, slapping, punching, pinching, choking, shoving, and restraining.

Verbal abuse is being aggressive in speech toward another person by using intimidation, humiliation, or manipulation. Examples are insulting, blaming, yelling, name-calling, bullying, foul language, belittling, berating, screaming in your face, threatening harm, threatening to commit suicide, threatening to report someone to the authorities, and derogatory statements.

Emotional/Mental/Psychological abuse is behavior that over time ruins or destroys another person's sense of identity, dignity, and self-worth, and often results in fear or anxiety. It is deliberately using words to manipulate, distort, confuse, hurt, weaken, or frighten a person mentally or emotionally. Examples are lying, gaslighting, excessive texting, constant monitoring, isolation, sleep interruptions, brainwashing, slanderous comments, causing embarrassment, destroying property, displaying weapons, abusing animals, and stalking.

Sexual abuse is forcing sexual behavior or taking advantage of someone in a sexual manner. Examples are making someone feel guilty for not wanting a sexual relationship, molestation, inappropriate touching, getting someone drunk or drugged to perform sex, rape, knowingly spreading sexually transmitted diseases, purposefully getting someone pregnant so they will stay, and pornography.

Financial abuse is controlling the financial resources of another, making them totally dependent. An example is one person not allowing another person access to bank accounts, checkbooks, or credit cards. By paying for everything, the abuser becomes the "boss" and only decision maker.

Physical abuse is terrible to endure, and it leaves bruises, scars, busted lips, and broken bones. These injuries can often tell the story of what has happened to the victim, but being physical, the actual injury will usually heal.

However, while the other types of abuse show no physical damage, the injuries to your inner person can be even more severe and last a lifetime. The non-physical abuses are more prevalent, but they are much less likely to be detected or even seen as abuse by the victims.

The self-talk which you are left with as your mind recalls the many scenes of abuse can repeat over and over and over. The experiences can grip onto every part of your soul. At all costs, avoid allowing these kinds of abuses to become part of your life experience.

Closely examine the individuals you trust into your world. Watch for the red flags. Someone may be setting a trap for you, and you could be caught innocently in their abusive web. You may greatly regret this later. Getting trapped may damage or destroy your mental and emotional health, impairing your future ability to socialize, work, parent, or otherwise function well in your day-to-day life. The impact may be very great, so do all you can to *AVOID THE TRAP!*

LESSON TWO:
*Watch with eyes wide open for the red flags that warn
you of dangerous traps ahead.*

Abusers often follow a pattern to manipulate and gain control over their victims. No one enters a relationship to be hurt, but many are tricked into testing the waters and missing all the red flags. At the beginning, there is often an intense "honeymoon" period, and abusers may be charming and affectionate, professing their love for you quickly and easily.

They may want you to spend all your time with them, while spending less and less time with your family and friends. Their jealousy may seem endearing to you, but over time you will find yourself isolated from others. Soon they will try to control who you can call, meet, or see.

Slowly they will desensitize you to their abusive behavior by insulting you, but claiming it was just a joke and you "misunderstood." There will be subtle blaming and picking at your faults. Sometimes they will try to convince you that you are mentally unstable by telling you different versions of the same incident and stating that you cannot remember anything accurately. Picking at your faults and starting arguments seem like normal behaviors to an abuser.

Gradually each small abuse increases in degree until you become more like a possession being required to obey than a loving partner and friend. Yet, at the same time, the abuser will often create emotional confusion by being kind and randomly doing nice things for short periods of time.

The abuser will use more and more tactics to make it difficult or impossible for the victim to escape their power and control. The victim may become completely trapped.

Some specific behaviors which should immediately indicate trouble ahead are:

• One hit of any kind is one too many! Do not allow another blow to happen. Remove yourself from this individual immediately, regardless of how charming they are or what they may have to offer! Tell a trusted person what happened to you. Promise yourself that you will not spend any more time with the abuser. Do not return to the abuser. If you do, the days and years ahead will just go on and on and on with intensifying abuse.

• Inability to communicate within normal boundaries; violent, explosive responses to daily life situations while driving, shopping, in restaurants or social situations. If a person lacks the social skills to control their behavior in public settings, they will certainly have less restraint in private situations. A person who has problems discussing differences on minor issues will certainly have problems discussing the bigger issues of life. You may want to talk things out, but it will be impossible.

• Addictive behaviors such as drinking, using drugs, and gambling

• Stalkerish behaviors such as being overbearing and jealous, not allowing any privacy, insisting on seeing your cell phone, texts, emails, or photos.

• Aggressive sexual behaviors such as forcing, threatening, or pressuring you into a sexual relationship. A person who will not take "No" as an answer has unhealthy relationship problems.

• Using you because you have something useful to them, such as money or resources. They will love you dearly if your resources are available to them, but when hard times come, they move on to someone else who can provide what they need.

• Significant mood swings which are not being treated medically. A pattern of aggressive and reckless behaviors or a history of violent behavior. A record of arrests for aggressive or disruptive behavior.

• Troubling relationships with their parents, siblings, close friends, or peers. Do you enjoy being with these people and do you share their values?

• Disapproval from your own family and friends concerning this relationship. Think twice before ignoring their disapproval of this individual. Reject having a secret relationship with them despite what your family and friends think. By having different life experiences, they may see problems ahead that you do not see.

Before you ever get deeply involved with an individual, take a close look at their behaviors and attitudes. Make an honest judgment as to what kind of person they are now. Do not rely on them changing to meet your expectations. At the same time, be honest with yourself on how you feel when you are with this person. Are you constantly "walking on eggshells" and avoiding physical or emotional blows? Or do you feel totally safe and secure?

One of the most hurtful parts of being in an abusive relationship is realizing that you were tricked into the relationship. It is common to feel completely shocked and blindsided by the abuser's toxic behavior. Many are totally mortified and do not want anyone to know what they are really going through.

It is impossible to comprehend that the person you love deeply and who says they love you as well would ever treat you in such a horrible way. That is totally shocking and devastating to your entire being because you never, ever, dreamed that something like this would happen to you.

Your self-worth and self-confidence are destroyed. Your dreams are shattered. You are left feeling totally trapped and miserable in a living nightmare and dangerous situation.

Please, please, please watch for the red flags when you enter new relationships.

LESSON THREE:
Stay as safe as possible while inside the danger zone.

Here are a few helpful hints to remember as you try to stay safe from further abuse once in a relationship with an abuser:

• Keep your cell phone always charged and accessible. Memorize important phone numbers.

• Have a list of important phone numbers hidden or given to a trusted friend, in case your phone is destroyed or stolen.

• Identify the safest areas of your house. Know the quickest path to any exits. Stay near doors when you are feeling threatened. Avoid getting trapped in small closets or bathrooms.

• Keep a spare set of keys hidden near the door for a quick exit.

• Have an extra set of keys hidden, in case the regular set has been taken away from you.

• Keep your car parked facing the street and filled with gas.

• Create plausible reasons for leaving the house alone, especially when trouble is brewing. Go get groceries, visit a needy friend, run to the post office, anything to get away for a while.

• Avoid wearing necklaces or scarves around your neck. They can be used to choke you.

• Stay away from steps and stairways when the abuser is present. You can be easily pushed down steps.

- Create verbal codes or visual clues with a few trusted individuals to indicate you are in trouble and need help.

- Get a will and power of attorney for the sake of your children.

- Get life insurance to provide for your children. List them as beneficiaries if you have insurance through your work.

- Try to keep working when possible. This gives you greater independence, a source of income, an excuse to need a vehicle and be away from home for long periods, peers to confide in, and someone to notice if you do not show up for work.

- Seek out counseling services or abuse groups on social media and the internet.

- Always stay alert. Avoid using drugs or medications that may interfere with your ability to respond quickly.

- Keep medications and supplies available to treat any injuries.

- Be involved with people and programs outside your home. Do activities you enjoy.

- Avoid confrontations and escalations as much as possible. Be aware of escalating conversations. Avoid power struggles and "fueling the fire." Attempt to diffuse escalating conversations.

- Teach your children to stay safe themselves and never try to protect you from the abuser. Teach them where to stay out of view from any confrontations.

• If violence is completely unavoidable and you are trapped in a room, move to a corner and curl into a ball as small as possible. Protect your face by putting your arms around each side of your head and entwine your fingers together.

• Contact the National Domestic Violence Hotline at 1-800-799-SAFE (1-800-799-7233) or www.the-hotline.org. Confidential and trained advocates are available 24/7 to help you develop a safety plan for you and your children.

• Contact the Teen Dating Abuse Helpline at 1-866-331-9474

LESSON FOUR:
Only escape when you have a safety plan.

I wish that I had left Mack and had gone where he could not find me, like California. But I was young, scared, had small children, and just did not know what to do. I stayed in my situation for far too long. I encourage anyone who has been tricked and trapped to escape if at all safely possible.

Why do people stay in abusive situations? That seems to be a reasonable question to people who are not personally involved. I have wondered that a lot myself, but over time I have come to realize that there are many, many valid reasons why people stay, including:

1. Victim fears serious injury or death by the abuser.

2. Victim fears children, pets, or extended family members could be taken, hurt, or killed by the abuser.

3. Victim lacks sufficient funds to pay for the expenses of leaving.

4. Victim has religious beliefs or a cultural background that frowns on divorce or separations from spouse.

5. Victim lacks support from family and friends; may have been isolated from that support by the abuser.

6. Victim lacks the physical ability to move (various disabilities)

7. Victim lacks a place to go; fears homelessness

8. Victim is young, naïve, vulnerable, clueless

9. Victim is under a deep fog from fear and shame; mentally confused or psychologically beaten down; paralyzed by fear

10. Victim fears that "no one else will want me." This is a lie often repeated to the victim by the abuser.

11. Victim believes the abuser's promise to never hurt them again. This is not true. Once the abuser starts physically hurting another person, it will happen again. An abuser has deep emotional and psychological problems which can only be resolved by intense, meaningful, and consistent psychological treatment. Very few abusers ever admit that they have been abusive, much less agree to working on their issues.

12. Victim has a background of parental abuse, so this seems like normal behavior

13. To the victim, the good times outweigh the bad times. The longer it goes, the worse it gets though.

14. Victim believes the abuser's "I love you," forgetting the pain that has been dealt over and over.

15. Victim has immigration status problems.

16. Victim's career could be impacted.

17. Victim could be shamed or embarrassed socially or in media.

18. Victim thinks and hopes the abuser will change. NO! Abusers frequently have deep emotional and psychological problems causing the abuse. Without an expressed desire from the abuser to change and a plan of action that is followed, a change will not occur. It is not possible for the victim to try enough, cry enough, work hard enough, or wait long enough for a change to happen. The victim has no power to change the abuser. That power is strictly within the abuser.

19. Victim believes they can "help" the abuser. NO! By staying and accepting repeated abuse, the victim reinforces and enables the abuser's behaviors. Staying does not "help." It can make the problem continue indefinitely.

20. Victim fears change. The unknown future is frightening and a plan for change is needed, but hard to formulate.

21. Victim minimizes the damage being done by the abuser, or even refuses to acknowledge that the injuries are abusive.

Clearly, there are many reasons why people stay, but fear is usually the root cause. To consider leaving and making a safe escape plan takes great courage.

The most dangerous time in an abusive relationship is when the victim leaves. On average, a person in an abusive relationship will try to leave about seven times before they are successful. Leaving can be extremely dangerous. Victims are 70 times more likely to be killed the two weeks after leaving their abuser than at any other time in the relationship.

It is of utmost importance that a plan for leaving is based on safety first. It could make the difference between being severely injured or killed and escaping with your life.

Here are a few safety tips that may be helpful if you are trapped, but wanting to escape:

• Carefully judge your abuser's level of force. How dangerous will leaving be?

• Record evidence of your abuse. Take photos. Keep a journal of violent incidents including dates, threats, injuries. Find a secret place to keep your journal or leave it with a trusted friend.

• When ready to leave, move or hide guns and kitchen knives from their normal storage areas.

• Contact the National Domestic Violence Hotline at 1-800-799-SAFE (1-800-799-7233) or www.the-hotline.org. Confidential and trained advocates are available 24/7 to help you develop a safety plan for you and your children.

• Contact local shelters and learn their locations and policies. Decide on the safest location to relocate.

• Tell a trusted friend you are planning to leave the relationship. Ask for help and advice. Discuss your plan with them.

• Create verbal codes or visual clues with a few trusted individuals to indicate you are in trouble and need help.

• Slowly and inconspicuously set aside small amounts of cash to use during your transition. Hide it well or ask a friend to keep it for you.

• Secure a small storage unit that is secured by gates and video camera with circular locks which cannot not be cut open. Quietly remove your valuables and important papers a little at a time.

• Be prepared that the abuser will want you to return to his control. Intense levels of persuasion may be used to convince you to come back:

--- "You are MINE (my girlfriend, my wife, my partner) and therefore I can do whatever I want, whenever I want. You need me. Besides no one else wants you!"

--- "I'm so, so sorry! I won't ever hurt you again! It won't happen again!" ... along with lots of sobs and crying.

--- "I love you so much, more than anyone else could ever love you!"

The abuser is such a manipulator and has lied so often that he believes his own lies. Regardless of his "sincerity," never believe him. No matter what, do not return.

LESSON FIVE:
Slowly recover and return to the person you once were.

For years I had dreamed of leaving Mack and all his abuse. I thought I would feel elated and free when I left. I thought I would walk away from the trauma and start all over again. I did not know that life "post-Mack" would be more like recovering from a major accident or surgery. It was a slow process, requiring a lot of support from others and hard work on my part. In the process, I learned how to feel safe again, how to deal with all the emotions I was experiencing, where to find support for my recovery, and eventually how to enjoy life again. It was a long journey back to feeling "normal" again and took much longer than I had expected.

Establish a safe environment

Once you leave your abuser, it is very import-ant to be in a safe place and for you to feel complete-ly safe. Here are some things you can do to improve your safety:

• Get a new phone number. Keep your cell phone charged, in your presence, and ready to call 911.

• Change all your joint passwords for your accounts and social media.

• Secure your home with additional locks and/or bars on the windows.

- Install motion sensitive lights and/or a security system.

- Never ever open your door unless you know for certain who is on the other side.

- Attempt to "disappear" and be very difficult to find.

- Change any appointments your abuser may know about.

- Rent a P.O. box instead of having your mail delivered to your new place.

- Change the hours you work and the routes you normally take to/from work.

- Change the stores/restaurants you usually use.

- Socialize in different circles.

- If your abuser shows up at your home or work and you feel frightened or threatened, call 911 immediately. Later you can go to the courthouse to file a restraining order. It costs nothing to fill it out and submit it. The restraining order requires your abuser to stop abusing and threatening you. Once submitted, it is illegal for your abuser to show up at your home or work. In some states it may even give you temporary custody of your children. Just be aware that in some situations this action can create danger for you, depending on the personality of your abuser. Mack continued to harass me even after I had the restraining order, but he did spend time in jail because of it.

Stabilize your emotions and self-esteem

- Be mindful that your emotions may be more intense than usual. Healing from trauma and abuse is a slow process. You possibly have been injured physically, mentally, and emotionally. Be very patient and gentle with yourself. There will be hard days and times of anxiety and fear. These times are very normal.

• Keep your self-talk positive. Remember that your abuser may have planted many negative thoughts in your mind. They were not necessarily true. No, your abuse was NOT your fault. No, you did NOT deserve the abuse. No, you are NOT crazy or weak. You are strong and can recover from the damage done by your abuser. Always remember that. Challenge any negative thoughts you have about yourself.

• It can be normal for you to feel sad, disappointed, and angry as you realize the losses that you experienced during the time you were being abused. You may even grieve for the lost relationship you had with your abuser.

• Work through some of your emotions by enjoying creative expressions that suit your personality. Keep a journal, write poetry, draw, do arts and crafts, sing, paint or do anything else that releases your creativity. Spend more time doing things you really enjoy doing. This is also a good time for you to try some new hobbies. Your new skills will help you feel stronger and more empowered. I took lessons on how to do flower arrangements and spent a lot of time reading. I also enjoyed doing various kinds of puzzle books.

• During times of abuse-related stress/anxiety, use deep breathing exercises to calm yourself. Being physically active by doing yoga, exercising at the gym, or taking long walks is also good for relieving stress.

Choose a positive activity, but absolutely avoid the temptation to use alcohol or drugs to dull your emotional pain. This will set back your recovery and can lead you down a dangerous path.

• A healthy self-esteem is being at peace with who you are and what you have to offer the world. It is accepting the person who you are and genuinely liking the person you have become through the recovery process. With a healthy self-esteem you will find yourself avoiding people who treat you disrespectfully. You will be able to set the boundaries of what is acceptable behavior by others.

Seek professional help

Remember that you are not alone in this recovery process. Besides trusted family members and friends, there are trained people and agencies waiting to help you with many resources. I went to a counselor for a while. Just being able to talk through everything with her helped a lot. Here are some resources you may find helpful:

• Contact local domestic abuse organizations in your local area. This website is searchable by state: https://www.thehotline.org/resources/victims-and-survivors/

• Join a local or online support group. It can be very helpful to share your experiences with someone who understands what you have been through because of their shared experiences. You can also give support to others in the group. For support, speak to someone at the National Domestic Abuse Hotline 1-800-799-7233.

• Make an appointment with your primary care giver who may be able to treat your symptoms of PTSD, anxiety, depression, anger issues, substance abuse, or eating disorders. You may also be referred to a therapist or counselor who specializes in trauma recovery. The American Psychological Association has a searchable database of psychologists by area if you would like to find one on your own at http://locator.apa.org.

• If you find that your emotions are spiraling out of control or if you are considering suicide, please reach out immediately to counselors who can help you anytime of the day or night. Call the National Suicide Prevention Hotline at 1-800-273-8255. Another free service available 24/7 is the Crisis Text Line. Just text TALK to 741-741 to reach a trained crisis counselor.

Remember, you are not alone. Reach out to any of these support agencies for help if you need it.

Take care of your body

It will be important to care for your body by consistently following these healthy habits:

• Get adequate sleep/rest (7-9 hours each night).

• Enjoy a well-balanced diet with lots of fruits and vegetables.

• Drink water frequently during the day to stay hydrated.

• Stay physically active. Begin with 10 minutes a day and grow to 30 minutes a day. Try walking, jogging, swimming, or dancing. Just keep moving.

- Focus on your personal hygiene and feel good about how you look.

You will know that your recovery is nearly complete when you are able to release the trauma to the past and keep it behind you. The abuse will no longer define your life. It will become just part of your story, not the only story. In all, be patient and do not hurry the process. Along the way you will reconnect with the core of who you are. Then you can create the life for yourself that you really want. Plan what you want and work toward your goals.

Recovery from domestic abuse does not happen overnight, but with time and support, it does happen.

A Glimmer of Hope

AFTERWORD

Always trust in the power of God to lead you through the darkest valleys of your life. I know the Lord helped me through all my terrible times. I asked God every day to keep me and my children safe. I know in my heart that if the Lord had not been with me, I would have been killed during my time with Mack. At the time, I felt like I had no feelings for myself or the outside world. The Lord, however, helped me stay sane through all those years of abuse and showed me a way to escape.

Although Mack is still part of my extended family with my children and grandchildren, I could never be close to him again. I behave politely around him when we are all together with our growing family. He still has a quick temper and seems angry much of the time.

I know that my children have been badly hurt through all the experiences they had growing up. I wish I could take the pain away from them, but that is not possible. All I can do is love them with all my heart and keep them in my prayers.

I also love the Lord with all my heart and soul. I know I can trust God completely. I ask Him to help me every day of my life. I pray for my family and my friends. I thank God that He brought me safely through those many years of heartaches and trials.

I thank God for the life and peace that I now enjoy. I thank Him for my apartment and for my loving church. Most of all, I thank God for my three children, my seven grandchildren, my twenty-two great-grandchildren, and my seven great-great-grandchildren. They are everything that is good in my life now. I am so blessed.

I pray that by reading about my experiences you will be able to avoid getting into a similar situation. If you are there already, I pray that you will find a way to escape and continue your life in a new direction. Remember that you are not to blame for having been abused, and you are not the cause of your abuser's behavior. You deserve to be treated with respect as you and your children live a safe and happy life.

Life is short and flies by quickly. Spend your days with the sunshine on your back and the peace of God in your heart. And always, always hold on to that little glimmer of hope that, just like the trapped caterpillar in his dark cocoon, God will bring you to a better day like a beautiful butterfly!

Warnock Pro on 50# LSI archival white
Type and Design by Karen Paul Stone

CPSIA information can be obtained
at www.ICGtesting.com
Printed in the USA
FSHW021344271021

9 781947 589469